THE
Parables
OF JESUS
PARTICIPANT'S GUIDE

D1042947

The Deeper Connections Series

The Miracles of Jesus

The Last Days of Jesus

The Forgiveness of Jesus

The Life of Jesus

The Parables of Jesus

The Prayers of Jesus

Deeper CONNECTIONS

THE
Parables
OF **JESUS**
PARTICIPANT'S GUIDE

Six In-depth Studies Connecting the Bible to Life

Matt Williams
General Editor

HENDRICKSON PUBLISHERS · ROSE PUBLISHING

Deeper Connections:
The Parables of Jesus Participant's Guide
© 2007, 2018 Matt Williams
Rose Publishing, LLC
P. O. Box 3473
Peabody, Massachusetts 01961-3473 USA
www.hendricksonrose.com

Download a free Leader's Guide at www.hendricksonrose.com/deeperconnections

All rights reserved. No part of this book may be reproduced or transmitted in any form or by any means, electronic or mechanical, including photocopying, recording, or by any information storage and retrieval system, without permission in writing from the publisher.

All Scripture quotations, unless otherwise indicated, are taken from the Holy Bible, New International Version ®. NIV®. Copyright © 1973, 1978, 1984 by International Bible Society. Used by permission of Zondervan. All rights reserved.

Rose Publishing is in no way liable for any context, change of content, or activity for the websites listed. Inclusion of a work does not necessarily mean endorsement of all its contents or of other works by the same author(s).

Interior Design: Mark Sheeres

Printed in the United States of America
September 2018, 2nd printing

Contents

Preface 7
About the Video Teachers 9

Session 1   The Coming of the Kingdom 11
Weeds, Mustard Seed, Yeast (Matthew 13:24–33)
Dr. Michael Wilkins

Session 2   The Grace of the Kingdom 31
Two Debtors (Luke 7:36–50)
Dr. Gary Burge

Session 3   The God of the Kingdom 49
The Prodigal Son (Luke 15:11–32)
Dr. Ben Witherington III

Session 4   The Demand of the Kingdom 69
Treasure and Pearls (Matthew 13:44–46)
Dr. David Garland

Session 5   The Mission of the Kingdom 85
The Wedding Banquet (Matthew 22:1–14)
Dr. Matt Williams

Session 6   The Fulfillment of the Kingdom 107
Sheep and Goats (Matthew 25:31–46)
Dr. Mark Strauss

Source Acknowledgments *129*
Map and Photo Credits *131*
Books for Further Reading *133*

Preface

We all know Christians who are bored with Bible study — not because the Bible is boring, but because they haven't been introduced to its meaning in its first-century context and how that is significant for our lives today. When we begin to understand some of these "deeper connections" — both to the first century and to the twenty-first century — our lives are transformed.

The idea for the Deeper Connections series grew out of a concern that far too many Bible studies lack depth and solid biblical application. We wanted a Bible study series that was written and taught by biblical experts who could also communicate that material in a *clear, practical, understandable* manner. The Deeper Connections teachers have one foot in the historical, biblical text and the other in the modern world; they not only have written numerous books, they have many years of pastoral experience. When they teach in the local church, they often hear comments such as, "Wow, I've never heard it explained that way before." Unfortunately that's because, until recently, Bible professors usually spent most of their time writing books for other professors or occasionally for pastors, and the layperson in the church had little access to this biblical knowledge. Deeper Connections seeks to remedy this by bringing the best in biblical scholarship directly to small groups and Sunday school classes through the popular medium of DVD.

Don't be scared by the word "deeper" — deeper does not mean that these studies are hard to understand. It simply means that we are attempting to get at the true meaning of the biblical text, which involves investigating the historical, religious, and social background of first-century Jewish culture and their Greek and Roman neighbors. If we fail to study and understand this background, then we also fail to understand the deeper and true meaning of the Bible.

After making deeper connections to the biblical texts, the teachers then apply that text to life in the twenty-first century. This is where a deeper look into the text really pays off. Life-application in the church today has sometimes been a bit shallow and many times unrelated to the biblical passage itself. In this series, the practical application derives directly out of the biblical text.

So, to borrow the alternate title of *The Hobbit*, J. R. R. Tolkien's bestselling classic, we invite you to join us on an adventure to "there and back again"! Your life won't be the same as a result.

About the Video Teachers

Dr. Gary Burge is professor of New Testament at Wheaton College in Wheaton, Illinois, and a sought-after conference speaker. His experiences in Beirut, Lebanon, in the early 1970s when civil war broke out have helped him to see how valuable it is to understand the world of the Middle East in order to correctly understand the biblical world of Jesus. Gary is the author of many books, including a commentary on the gospel of John.

Dr. David Garland is professor of Christian Scriptures at Truett Theological Seminary, Baylor University, Waco, Texas. David is closely connected to local church ministry and has served as interim pastor of fifteen churches in Kentucky, Indiana, and Texas. He is the author of many books, including commentaries on the gospels of Matthew and Mark.

Dr. Mark Strauss is professor of New Testament at Bethel Seminary in San Diego, California. He is a frequent preacher at San Diego area churches and has served in three interim pastorates. Mark is the author of many books, including a commentary on the gospel of Luke and *Four Portraits, One Jesus: An Introduction to Jesus and the Gospels*.

Dr. Michael Wilkins is professor of New Testament Language and Literature and the dean of the faculty at Talbot School of Theology, Biola University, La Mirada, California. Michael speaks throughout the world about his two passions: surfing and discipleship. He was senior pastor of two different churches in California and has written numerous books, including two commentaries on the gospel of Matthew.

Dr. Matt Williams is associate professor of New Testament at Talbot School of Theology, Biola University, La Mirada, California. A former missionary to Spain, Matt preaches and teaches at churches throughout the United States and Spain. He is general editor of *Colección Teológica Contemporánea*, a series of theological books in Spanish, and is the author of two books on the Gospels.

Dr. Ben Witherington III is professor of New Testament at Asbury Theological Seminary in Wilmore, Kentucky. Ben is an avid fan of jazz and sports, especially the Atlanta Braves. He has led numerous study tours through the lands of the Bible and is known for bringing the text to life through incisive historical and cultural analysis. He is a prolific author, including commentaries on all four gospels.

Host **Jarrett Stevens** is director of the college and singles ministry and teacher for 7/22 at North Point Church in Alpharetta, Georgia. Prior to that he was on staff at Willow Creek Community Church in suburban Chicago.

The Coming of the Kingdom

Weeds, Mustard Seed, Yeast (Matthew 13:24–33)

Dr. Michael Wilkins

"The owner's servants came to him and said, 'Sir, didn't you sow good seed in your field? Where then did the weeds come from?' "

Matthew 13:27

One day God's causes will triumph.

Craig Blomberg

INTRODUCTION

Video Opener

Scripture Reading: Matthew 13:24–33, followed by a prayer that God will open your heart as you study his Word

Location of Parable: Capernaum, along Sea of Galilee, near Peter's home

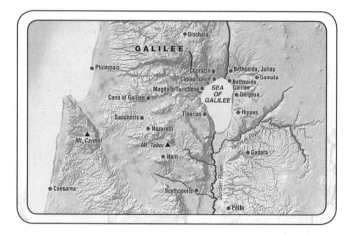

Ruins of Peter's home in foreground

CONNECTING TO THE BIBLE

The kingdom is now present with the arrival of the messianic king. But some of what the Jewish people expected to happen immediately — especially full judgment and restoration — awaits future final fulfillment.

Video Teaching #1 Notes

Location of Video Teaching: Tanaka Farms, Irvine, California

"Repent, for the kingdom of heaven is near" (Matthew 4:17)

Jewish expectations of the kingdom

The Zealots tried to bring the kingdom through violence; Qumran tried by separating from the "impure." Even Jesus' disciples wanted immediate judgment of the unrighteous by "call[ing] fire down from heaven" (Luke 9:51–56, especially v. 54).

Jesus fulfilled Old Testament prophecies differently than expected

Though John the Baptist talked about a coming judgment (Matthew 3:7–12), these parables teach us that the judgment will be delayed until "the end of the age."

The parable of the wheat and the weeds (Matthew 13:24–30, 36–43)

"The kingdom of heaven is like a man who sowed good seed in his field."

Matthew 13:24

The good seed

DID YOU KNOW?

To sow darnel among wheat as an act of revenge was punishable by Roman law.

R. T. France

The bad seed

Farmer lets both grow together

While the victory of God's kingdom is sure, the way from here to there is hampered by unbelief and its effects.

W. D. Davies and Dale Allison

The parable of the mustard seed (Matthew 13:31–32)

"The kingdom of heaven is like a mustard seed, which a man took and planted in his field."

Matthew 13:31

Mustard seeds

In the kingdom, great results stem from small beginnings.

Robert Mounce

The parable of the yeast (Matthew 13:33)

"The kingdom of heaven is like yeast that a woman took and mixed into a large amount [sixty pounds] of flour until it worked all through the dough."

Matthew 13:33

DID YOU KNOW?

Bread made with yeast was known as "leavened," as distinct from bread that was baked with no yeast, which was known as "unleavened."

Unleavened bread (matzah)

Would the people have understood what Jesus was trying to teach them about the kingdom of God?

VIDEO DISCUSSION #1

1. Looking back at the Bible passage and your video teaching notes, what did you learn that you did not know previously? Consider specifically:

   • Jewish expectations of the kingdom

   • Jesus did not fulfill those expectations the way the Jews had hoped

   • The different seeds and/or yeast

   • The meaning of one of the parables

   How does this knowledge help you to understand the passage better?

2. Imagine that you were a Jewish person living in the first century as Jesus taught about the kingdom of God through these parables. Do you think that you would have understood what Jesus was trying to say, given the Jewish expectations of the immediate coming of the kingdom in all of its fullness? Why or why not?

GOING DEEPER

When Jesus announced that "the kingdom was near," most people would have thought of their current oppression by Rome and their need for political freedom.

Video Teaching #2 Notes

Jewish texts about the coming kingdom

The promise to King David

"But you, O Israel, my servant . . . do not fear, for I am with you; do not be dismayed, for I am your God. I will strengthen you and help you; I will uphold you with my righteous right hand. All who rage against you will surely be ashamed and disgraced; those who oppose you will be as nothing and perish. Though you search for your enemies, you will not find them."

Isaiah 41:8, 10–12

The expectation of a kingly Davidic Messiah

Judas Maccabeus (c.190 –160 BC)

> "Judas Maccabeus has been a mighty warrior from his youth; he shall command the army for you.... Pay back the Gentiles in full, and obey the commands of the law." Then his son Judas, who was called Maccabeus, took command.... He searched out and pursued those who broke the law; he burned those who troubled his people.... He went through the cities of Judah; he destroyed the ungodly out of the land.
>
> 1 Maccabees 2:66 –3:8

Will Jesus fight Rome?

The explanation of the parable of the wheat and weeds (Matthew 13:36 –43)

The **sower** of the good seed is Jesus.

The **good seed** are the people of the kingdom.

The **bad weeds** are those who reject the gospel message.

The **evil one** is the Devil.

The **field** is the world.

The **harvest** is the judgment.

The **harvesters** are identified as angels.

The interpretation of the parables of the mustard seed and the yeast

The kingdom rules hearts

The kingdom begins small

The kingdom will be visible

Over against the mighty numbers of the worshipers of heathen gods, those who proclaimed the kingdom were a tiny minority. Jesus teaches them not to be hypnotized by size.

Leon Morris

VIDEO DISCUSSION #2

1. Given Jewish background and history, why do you think that most Jews expected a physical liberator who would bring them physical freedom rather than spiritual freedom? Do you think that Jesus brought physical or spiritual freedom in his ministry?

2. Given that other "Messiah" figures existed around the time of Jesus, such as Judas Maccabeus, do you think it would have been easy or hard for the Jewish people to believe that Jesus was the true Messiah? Explain.

3. Do you think that it would have been surprising for the Jewish people to hear that the "enemy" of the farmer was not Rome, but the Devil (Matthew 13:39)? Why?

CONNECTING THE BIBLE TO LIFE

Though Jesus began the enemy's overthrow by inaugurating the kingdom of God, the world still lies in the enemy's grip. As disciples, we now continue this battle in our own lives.

Video Teaching #3 Notes

We are undercover agents of God's kingdom

The kingdom is unseen, but is powerful to transform us

> From a distance Jesus' disciples may not look different from others in this world, but there is an inherent difference as a result of the transformation that is produced by the impact of the kingdom of heaven in a person's life. The wheat of the kingdom of heaven are "good" (Matthew 13:38) and "righteous" (v. 43).
>
> Michael Wilkins

The battle with the Evil One continues

We need to be gently intolerant of sin

Italian sculpture of Jesus and Judas

The kingdom of God will remain hidden and inconspicuous

The church has experienced remarkable growth at various periods of time in the world's history, but often at the expense of contamination from the world.

Michael Wilkins

Expect powerful transformation

"They will glimmer like the sun" (Matthew 13:43) [are] almost exactly the same words used in describing the transfiguration of Jesus in 17:2. This suggests that we will experience the glory of God.

Donald Hagner

I want to live the reality of the kingdom of God in Jesus' way and not mine, and then wait for his coming in glory to establish his kingdom in its final form at the end of the age.

Michael Wilkins

VIDEO DISCUSSION #3

1. Living in the midst of evil, does it bring you any comfort that one day the Son of Man will bring justice to the "bad seed" (Matthew 13:40–42)? What difference does this knowledge make in your daily life?

2. Do you think that the truth found in Jesus' parables — that the kingdom is hidden but powerful — is being lived out in your life? In the church today? Why or why not?

3. What does it mean not to allow weeds to grow in the church? How can we avoid weeds in our own lives?

MAKING DEEPER CONNECTIONS IN YOUR OWN LIFE

Personal reflection studies to do on your own

Day One

1. Read John 14:15–21; 17:9–20.

2. Even though the parables in Matthew 13 bring "bad" news by showing us that the full manifestation of the kingdom will not come until the end of the age (v. 39), there is some good news: Jesus has promised that he will pray for our protection from the Devil (John 17:15). What difference does it make in your life to know that Jesus is praying for you?

3. Jesus also sent the Holy Spirit (John 14:16), whose task it is to empower us to transform our lives in this evil world. (See Ephesians 3:16: "I pray that out of his glorious riches he may strengthen you with power through his Spirit in your inner being.") Are you relying on your own strength or on the strength of the Lord to be transformed? How?

Day Two

1. Read Matthew 3:2; Revelation 21:1–5.

2. The Matthew 13 parables teach us that the kingdom is here, but not fully. It has been inaugurated but not consummated, started but not completed. We must keep both of these elements in balance in our understanding of Christianity. An overemphasis on the "now-ness" of the kingdom (miracles, healings, victory over sin) can cause us to despair when we realize God does not manifest the truth of his reign over everything at this time. As you reflect on the now-ness of the kingdom, how might you practically acknowledge it in your daily life?

3. On the other hand, overemphasis on the "not-yet-ness" of the kingdom of God can cause feelings of helplessness and despair when we realize our insufficiency to defeat sin, transform the church, experience the power of the kingdom, and so on. This may lead to a lack of the joy and victory which Jesus promised (Matthew 16:18). Reflect on the nature of the not-yet-ness of the kingdom. What can you do to keep a balance between the now and not-yet aspects of the kingdom?

Day Three

1. Read 1 Peter 5:8–11; Revelation 12:10–12.

2. We know that Satan's plan is to plant evil seeds to infiltrate this world (Matthew 13:30, 38–39). Recognizing that he will also attempt to infiltrate the church, we need to protect our churches against sinful activities which give him a foothold (Ephesians 4:27) and deal effectively and quickly with sin in the body when it does occur (Matthew 18:15–20). Spend some time praying for your church and its leaders, examining your own heart to make sure that no stumbling blocks exist between you and another member of your church community. Journal any insights.

3. Christians — especially those in ministry — ought to be careful to watch over fellow Christians, fully aware that tares still grow among the wheat in this inaugurated kingdom and can make their way into church. Consider a fellow believer or two who you can watch over or "shepherd" so that they do not fall prey to the Evil One.

Day Four

1. Read Revelation 21:6–8.

2. The parable of the wheat and the tares reminds us of the reality of judgment (Matthew 13:40–42). Do we today sense the

urgency of the judgment for those who do not believe? What are we doing about it? What could we be doing about it?

3. Matthew 13:25 says that the enemy came and planted the bad seed while "everyone was sleeping." While this detail might be insignificant, it brings to mind the necessity for us Christians to be awake, fully alert to the strategies of the Evil One. Pray that God would give you insight into the enemy's plans to thwart your Christian growth. Pray for the power to resist his temptations (Matthew 6:13).

Day Five

1. Read Matthew 13:24–33 one more time.

2. Pray through the entire passage verse by verse, allowing the deeper meaning that you have discovered to lead you as you pray. Ask the Spirit to continue to remind you of what you have learned and to help you apply these truths to your life.

3. Turn back to the discussion questions from the video teaching (Video Discussion #1, #2, #3). If there are questions that your group did not have time to discuss or questions that you might like to think more about, use this time to review and reflect further.

The Grace of the Kingdom

Two Debtors
(Luke 7:36–50)

Dr. Gary Burge

"Her many sins have been forgiven — for she loved much."

Luke 7:47

No matter how many and how great the sins, God's grace can forgive them.

Leon Morris

INTRODUCTION

Video Opener

Scripture Reading: Luke 7:36–50, followed by a prayer that God will open your heart as you study his Word

Location of Parable: Somewhere in Galilee, perhaps near Nain (Luke 7:11), nine miles southeast of Nazareth

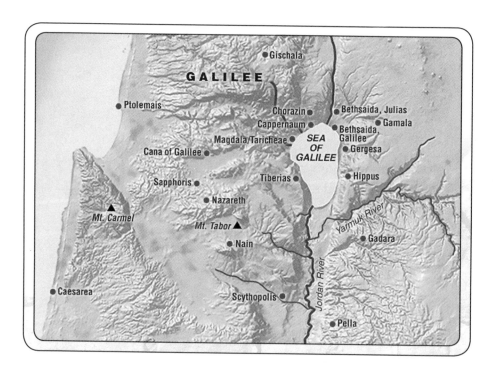

CONNECTING TO THE BIBLE

Jesus' world was populated by a wide range of people. Some were faithful to Judaism while others lived on the religious margins. But Jesus loved these people on the margin and tried to reach them with the grace of God.

Video Teaching #1 Notes

Location of Video Teaching: Lake Michigan, Chicago

Religious people in Jesus' world

People on the margin in Jesus' world

Jesus' reputation was widespread

Invited to Simon's home

DID YOU KNOW?

The invitation indicates that Simon views Jesus as a social equal, that is, a respected rabbi.

Mark Strauss

One of the Pharisees invited Jesus to have dinner with him, so he went to the Pharisee's house and reclined at the table.

Luke 7:36

The three ritual greetings in Jesus' day

Jesus is not greeted — publicly offended

"I came into your house. You did not give me any water for my feet. . . . You did not give me a kiss. . . . You did not put oil on my head."

Luke 7:44 – 46

The woman

Luke often introduces persons into the narrative who have already begun the journey of discipleship though we are never told when or how.

Joel Green

The woman anoints Jesus

Alabastar jar

When a woman who had lived a sinful life in that town learned that Jesus was eating at the Pharisee's house, she brought an alabaster jar of perfume, and as she stood behind him at his feet weeping, she began to wet his feet with her tears. Then she wiped them with her hair, kissed them and poured perfume on them.

Luke 7:37–38

Simon's choice

> "If this man were a prophet, he would know who is touching him and what kind of woman she is — that she is a sinner."
>
> Luke 7:39

The form of the sentence in Greek implies that Simon did not think that (a) Jesus was a prophet and (b) Jesus knew what sort of woman was touching him.

Leon Morris

Jesus' choice

VIDEO DISCUSSION #1

1. Looking back at the Bible passage and your video teaching notes, what did you learn that you did not know previously? Consider specifically:

   • People on the margins in Jesus' day

   • Ritual greetings in Jesus' day

   • Simon's intentions

   • Jesus' dilemma as one who wants to show grace, while not showing an acceptance of a sinful lifestyle

   • Male/female boundaries in that culture

   How does this knowledge help you to understand the passage better?

2. Gary Burge said that Jesus was in a dilemma between showing grace to this woman and taking the law and sin seriously. Have you found it difficult to find the balance between taking the law of God seriously while also treating others (and yourself) with grace? Explain an example from your life to the group.

GOING DEEPER

Religious leaders in Jesus' day formed societies where men sat in the evenings, ate meals, discussed the important matters of village life, and debated theology. Sinners and women were normally not welcome at such gatherings.

Video Teaching #2 Notes

The room or courtyard

At special meals the door was left open, so uninvited guests could enter, sit by the walls, and hear the conversation.

Darrell Bock

The table — the Roman triclinium

DID YOU KNOW?

People reclined on low couches at festive meals, leaning on the left arm with the head towards the table and the body stretched away from it. The sandals were removed before reclining. The woman was thus able to approach Jesus' feet without difficulty.

Leon Morris

Jesus is not greeted: a major offense

The rescue by the woman

Possible misunderstanding of the woman's character

Any woman with her hair exposed to public view would be considered promiscuous.

Craig Keener

Jesus does not reject the woman

Simon does not understand Jesus

> She does not [now] need forgiveness from God, but she does need recognition of her new life and forgiveness among God's people.
>
> Joel Green

Jesus' parable

DID YOU KNOW?

A denarius was a Roman coin equivalent to about a day's wages for a laborer.

Mark Strauss

"Two men owed money to a certain moneylender. One owed him five hundred denarii, and the other fifty. Neither of them had the money to pay him back, so he canceled the debts of both. Now which of them will love him more?"

Luke 7:41– 42

Jesus' dramatic announcement

"Therefore, I tell you, her many sins have been forgiven — for she loved much."

Luke 7:47

Verse 47: Grace and good works

Jesus is not saying that the woman's action had earned forgiveness, nor even that her love had merited it. . . . He is saying that her love is proof that she had already been forgiven.

Leon Morris

VIDEO DISCUSSION #2

1. Do you see yourself as having been forgiven by Jesus of 50 or 500 denarii? What difference has this realization made in your life, especially in how you treat others?

2. Why do you think that Gary Burge was so concerned about translating Luke 7:47 correctly, especially the meaning of the word "for"?

CONNECTING THE BIBLE TO LIFE

If we forget what it means to be forgiven by God, it will be evident in our lives.

Video Teaching #3 Notes

Recap of story

Jesus' grace and compassion

Simon

The woman

VIDEO DISCUSSION #3

1. If someone were to walk into your church, would they be more likely to run into a person like Simon or like Jesus?

2. In your response to Jesus, are you more like Simon or the woman? Why?

3. Simon's life was closed, proud, self-satisfied, and religious. The woman was a remarkable "sinner" and yet — there is something here that sets her apart. What are the attributes that Jesus sees in the woman, and how might we imitate them?

MAKING DEEPER CONNECTIONS IN YOUR OWN LIFE

Personal reflection studies to do on your own

Day One

1. Read Luke 7:47–50.

2. If we have forgotten what it means to be forgiven by God, it will be evident in our lives when we find it difficult to forgive others who wrong us. Reflect on your relationships with other people. Do you have difficulty offering forgiveness to others? Why or why not? How are the Christians in your city and in your church doing in this area?

3. Gary Burge said in the video teaching that Simon was a "religious person." Have there been times when you felt like you were just going through the religious motions (going to church, praying, reading your Bible, fellowship, ministry, and so on) and had forgotten your need for personal forgiveness and a personal relationship with Jesus? If so, how did you get back on spiritual track?

Day Two

1. Read Matthew 26:6–13, noting the similarities to and differences from Luke 7:36–50.

2. This incident tells us much about the person of Jesus. As a human being, he showed this woman grace and compassion, but the fact that he was actually able to do something about her sins — forgive them — tells us that he was also divine (Luke 7:48, see also 5:24). As Christians, it is important that we equally value both the human and divine aspects of Jesus' character. If you tend to overvalue one aspect at the expense of the other, which is it and why?

3. According to the Luke 7 account, the woman does not say a single word. Nor does she anoint Jesus' head, as would have been normal, but his feet. This is not only an act of devotion, but of humility (v. 46). Simon, on the other hand, seems to exude pride in his life (v. 39). Read Luke 14:11 and reflect on times in your own life when you have been overcome by pride versus times when you acted in humility. How did God convict you of prideful behavior? In what ways, if any, did he reward your humility?

4. Read again the verses of the parable Jesus told in Luke 7:41–42. How does Jesus tie the parable to the woman's actions and Simon's inaction (vv. 44–47)? What evidences in your life show your love for God?

Day Three

1. Read Mark 14:1–11, noting the similarities to and differences from Luke 7:36–50.

2. The woman's grateful heart led her to perform acts of devotion toward Jesus (Luke 7:44–47). Reflect on your life: are you grateful? Does your gratefulness lead you to acts of worship toward God? Describe them.

3. According to the Luke passage, Jesus tells the woman that it was her faith that "saved" her (7:50). How do you understand the relationship between faith and works (7:47)? Can one have faith without works? Can one have works without faith? See Ephesians 2:8–10 and James 2:14–26 for other Scripture references about faith and works.

Day Four

1. Read John 12:1–8, noting the similarities to and differences from Luke 7:36–50.

2. One of the main problems that Simon had with Jesus is that he allowed this "sinner" to get physically close to him (Luke 7:39).

More than twenty-five years ago Rebecca Pippert wrote a book, *Out of the Saltshaker*, in which she called for Christians to get out of the church so that they could have contact with the world — not to be contaminated by the world, but to reach the world with the forgiveness of Jesus. Do you think that the church in your area is "in" or "out" of the saltshaker? What are the advantages and disadvantages of both? What about you — are you out of the saltshaker so that you can influence your world (Matthew 5:13)?

3. Who could you reach out to with God's forgiveness? How might you start the process?

Day Five

1. Read Luke 7:36–50 one more time.

2. Pray through the entire passage verse by verse, allowing the deeper meaning that you have discovered to lead you as you pray. Ask the Spirit to continue to remind you of what you have learned and to help you apply these truths to your life.

3. Turn back to the discussion questions from the video teaching (Video Discussion #1, #2, #3). If there are questions that your group did not have time to discuss or questions that you might like to think more about, use this time to review and reflect further.

The God of the Kingdom

The Prodigal Son
(Luke 15:11–32)

Dr. Ben Witherington III

"This son of mine was dead and is alive again; he was lost and is found."

Luke 15:24

This parable illustrates the nature of God's freely offered love and tells of its cost. It is a love that seeks and suffers in order to save.

Kenneth Bailey

INTRODUCTION

Video Opener

Scripture Reading: Luke 15:11–32, followed by a prayer that God will open your heart as you study his Word

Location of Parable: Exact location unknown (Luke 11:1); probably in Galilee, as Jesus is on his way to Jerusalem (9:51), preaching in small towns and villages (13:22)

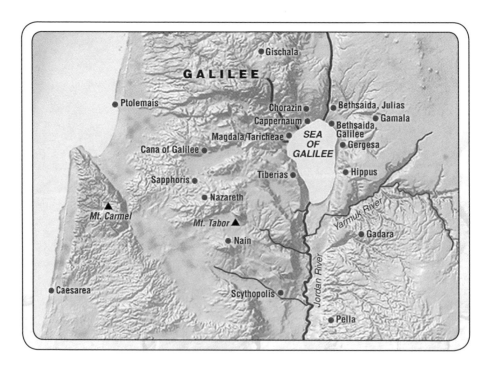

CONNECTING TO THE BIBLE

This is a parable about the character of God and the lostness of humanity — about a Father who is willing to go out to those who make even a step in the right direction.

Video Teaching #1 Notes

Location of Video Teaching: Gloucester Harbor, Gloucester, Massachusetts

The story of the prodigal son

The younger brother demands his inheritance and squanders it in a faraway country

> The younger one said to his father, "Father, give me my share of the estate."
>
> Luke 15:12

DID YOU KNOW?

Pigs were unclean animals for Jews (Leviticus 11:7; Deuteronomy 14:8) and to tend them was viewed as despicable work.

Mark Strauss

To liquidate his portion of the estate and then to leave his family amounted to an act of the grossest disregard and disloyalty.

Craig Evans

Turning point: "When he came to his senses"

"When he came to his senses, he said, '. . . I will set out and go back to my father and say to him: Father, I have sinned against heaven and against you. I am no longer worthy to be called your son; make me like one of your hired men.' So he got up and went to his father."

Luke 15:17–20

"Came to his senses" was a common idiom, which in this Jewish story may carry the Semitic idea of repentance.

Walter Liefeld

The father's reaction to his son's return

But while he was still a long way off, his father saw him and was filled with compassion for him; he ran to his son, threw his arms around him and kissed him.

Luke 15:20

The father throws a party

The fatted calf is more significant in first-century Palestine than it might appear to us, since meat was normally eaten only on special festive occasions (normally religious).

John Nolland

The older brother's reaction to the son's return

DID YOU KNOW?

According to Middle Eastern custom, the oldest son should have been the key reconciler between the father and his rebellious sibling.

Mark Strauss

"All these years I've been slaving for you and never disobeyed your orders. Yet you never gave me even a young goat so I could celebrate with my friends. But when this son of yours who has squandered your property with prostitutes comes home, you kill the fattened calf for him!"

Luke 15:29–30

The father's reaction to the older son's complaint

"My son," the father said, "you are always with me, and everything I have is yours. But we had to celebrate and be glad, because this brother of yours was dead and is alive again; he was lost and is found."

Luke 15:31–32

A parable: relationships between God the Father and his sons

VIDEO DISCUSSION #1

1. Looking back at the Bible passage and your video teaching notes, what did you learn that you did not know previously? Consider specifically:

   • What it meant to demand your inheritance in that culture

   • What it meant for the father to run in that culture

   • The older brother's response at the return of his brother

   • The character of the father (God) in his response to the two sons

   How does this knowledge help you to understand the parable better?

2. Read the context of this parable in Luke 15:1–2. Thinking about the cultural and religious situation surrounding Jesus' ministry, who do the father and the younger son represent? Why do you think the "elder brother" in this parable is upset? What is Jesus trying to teach his listeners through this parable about his own ministry?

GOING DEEPER

One of the great dangers with a beloved parable like the one about the prodigal son is that we think we know what it means, but we don't see it in the larger framework in which it was given.

Video Teaching #2 Notes

Legal context

> By asking for his portion of the inheritance, the younger son is saying to his father, "I wish you were dead."
>
> Kenneth Bailey

Honor-shame culture

> ### DID YOU KNOW?
>
> The Jews considered the loss of family property to Gentiles a particularly grievous offense and grounds for excommunication.
>
> Mark Strauss

> The son has shamed not only his father but the entire community. They would then perform the qesasah ceremony, in which they would break a jar in the street and excommunicate him from the entire village.
>
> Kenneth Bailey

The older brother is upset

> "The older brother became angry and refused to go in. So his father went out and pleaded with him."
>
> Luke 15:28

How would this parable be heard in the first century?

The older brother represents . . .

The prodigal and the elder brother of the parable are to be linked on the one hand to the tax collectors and sinners and on the other hand to the Pharisees and scribes of vv. 1–2.

John Nolland

The younger brother represents . . .

The father represents . . .

DID YOU KNOW?

A Middle Eastern patriarch in robes does not run, but always walks in a slow and dignified manner. Running was viewed as humiliating and degrading.

Mark Strauss

The ring would probably be a family signet ring — a symbol of reinstatement to sonship in a well-to-do house.

Craig Keener

The nature of the kingdom of God

VIDEO DISCUSSION #2

1. Given that the younger son is shaming his father by asking for his inheritance, why do you think the father grants him his request? What does this tell us about God?

2. Given that the younger son has shamed his father and the entire village, why do you think that the father accepts his son back, especially given that in the first-century context the normal response to such an action would be excommunicating the son from all village life? What does this tell us about God? What does it tell us about our own relationship with God, especially when we are "prone to wander"?

CONNECTING THE BIBLE TO LIFE

The story of the prodigal son is even more the story of the forgiving father.

Video Teaching #3 Notes

The character of God

The love expressed by the Father is too profound for words.

Kenneth Bailey

Forgiveness

> Then Peter came to Jesus and asked, "Lord, how many times shall I forgive my brother when he sins against me? Up to seven times?" Jesus answered, "I tell you, not seven times, but seventy-seven times."
>
> Matthew 18:21–22
>
> ❦
>
> "If Cain is avenged seven times, then Lamech seventy-seven times."
>
> Genesis 4:24

The reception of forgiveness

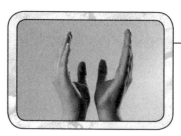

> "Father, I have sinned against heaven and against you. I am no longer worthy to be called your son; make me like one of your hired men."
>
> Luke 15:18 – 19

The church

Repentance

Repentance should be seen as acceptance of grace and the confession
of unworthiness.

Kenneth Bailey

The statue in Gloucester
Harbor

Emblem of the Father

Emblem of the church

Christ has no hands but our hands to do his work today, he has no feet but our feet to lead us in his way . . . he has no help but our help to bring them to his side.

Mother Teresa

VIDEO DISCUSSION #3

1. How does this parable change your image of who God is and how he acts in the world?

2. Ben Witherington said that the statue of the woman with her children looking out to sea awaiting her husband is a powerful image both of our Father God, who waits for his wayward children to return to him, and the church, whose job it is to reach these wayward children. Do you think that the people in your church community are looking "out to sea" for the lost in your community to come to God? Why or why not?

3. Do you know anyone who is presently living in a far-off land ("distant country," Luke 15:13)? Have you given up hope that they will return to the waiting arms of the Father? Spend some time as a group praying for those that you know who need to return.

MAKING DEEPER CONNECTIONS IN YOUR OWN LIFE

Personal reflection studies to do on your own

Day One

1. Read Luke 15:11–32.

2. In the parable of the prodigal son, do you relate more to the older brother, the younger brother, or the father? Why?

3. Chris Tomlin sings a song, "Come Home Running," whose lyrics include: "You've been too long out on your own, and he's been there all along, watching for you down the road. So, come home running, his arms are open wide. His name is Jesus; he understands." Do you fear God or do you go home to him, knowing that he is waiting for you with open arms of forgiveness? Spend some time praying, enjoying the embrace of the Father.

Day Two

1. Read Romans 5:8–11.

2. Kenneth Bailey (Poet and Peasant, p. 182) thinks that the Father runs to the son because he wants to reach him before the son enters the village and faces humiliation from a village that has

excommunicated him. In what way(s) has God taken away your humiliation and shame by forgiving you?

3. Consider the price that the father had to pay to reconcile with his son in this parable — the shame that he brought upon himself in that culture by running to accept back this wayward young man. Now think about the shame that Jesus willingly bore to reconcile us to God. Thank him for this great act of sacrificial love.

Day Three

1. Read Luke 15:1–7.

2. Luke 15:24 says that the father and townspeople began to "celebrate" the return of the younger son. Though the text does not use the term "joy," the idea is certainly in the context of Luke 15 (see vv. 5, 6, 9, 10, 32). Spend some time thinking and praying about the idea that the God of the universe rejoices over YOU (see Zephaniah 3:17: "The LORD your God is with you, he is mighty to save. He will take great delight in you, he will quiet you with his love, he will rejoice over you with singing").

3. Read Romans 8:15–17 where the apostle Paul writes that we are heirs of God and that as his children, we do not need to fear. Surely the prodigal son experienced great fear as he journeyed home. Do you have an excess of fear in your life? Write briefly what you imagine it must feel like to rest in the Father's arms.

Day Four

1. Read Luke 15:8–10.

2. The older son in the parable did not rejoice that his brother had returned. He represents those Jewish people in Jesus' day who refused to accept the repentance of sinners. What is your attitude toward those who come to the church from sinful backgrounds? Do you welcome them back, or do you stay outside questioning the Father as to why he accepts these people?

3. Reflect on the relationship between repentance and forgiveness. Some think that the Father accepts all, with no need for repentance. Do you agree with that line of thought or not? What Bible texts would you cite in response to someone who says that repentance is not needed to be forgiven by God?

Day Five

1. Read Luke 15:11–32 one more time.

2. Pray through the entire passage verse by verse, allowing the deeper meaning that you have discovered to lead you as you pray. Ask the Spirit to continue to remind you of what you have learned and to help you apply these truths to your life.

3. Turn back to the discussion questions from the video teaching (Video Discussion #1, #2, #3). If there are questions that your group did not have time to discuss or questions that you might like to think more about, use this time to review and reflect further.

The Demand of the Kingdom

Treasure and Pearls (Matthew 13:44–46)

Dr. David Garland

"The kingdom of heaven is like treasure hidden in a field. When a man found it, he hid it again, and then in his joy went and sold all he had and bought that field."

Matthew 13:44

We are called to sacrifice all for the kingdom, but, paradoxically, we also find in the kingdom all we need.

Donald Hagner

INTRODUCTION

Video Opener

Scripture Reading: Matthew 13:44–46, followed by a prayer that God will open your heart as you study his Word

Location of Parable: Capernaum, along Sea of Galilee, near Peter's home

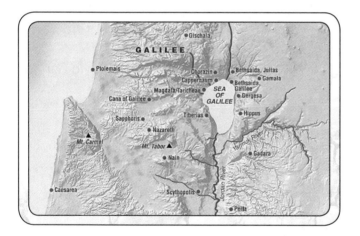

Ruins of Peter's home in foreground

CONNECTING TO THE BIBLE

The treasure trove motif fascinates people across all cultures — being able to strike it rich by discovering a buried treasure or a gold vein.

Video Teaching #1 Notes

Location of Video Teaching: Colorado Rockies

Parable #1: treasure in the field

> ### DID YOU KNOW?
>
> The Copper Scroll found at Qumran (Dead Sea Scrolls) lists sixty-four places in Palestine where treasures were apparently hidden.

Buried treasure in Jesus' day

The questionable ethics of the hired hand

A rabbinical story about honesty

Parable #2: pearl of great price

"Again, the kingdom of heaven is like a merchant looking for fine pearls. When he found one of great value, he went away and sold everything he had and bought it."

Matthew 13:45–46

The point is not about buying one's way into the kingdom but about recognizing its supreme value.

Michael Wilkins

VIDEO DISCUSSION #1

1. Looking back at the Bible passage and your video teaching notes, what did you learn that you did not know previously? Consider specifically:

   • The possibility of finding buried treasure in Palestine

   • The "shady" practices of the hired hand

   • The value of pearls in the first century

   How does this knowledge help you to understand the parables better?

2. Why do you think these people sold everything they had in order to purchase the land or the pearl? From what Jesus said in Matthew 13:44–46, do you think that it was a hard decision for them to make?

GOING DEEPER

We in the twenty-first century think that the treasure must belong to the owner of the field, but this is not the way it would have been perceived in the time of Jesus.

Video Teaching #2 Notes

The rabbis had rules for ownerless property

To acquire ownerless property, one had to move it

The field hand must take a bold course of action

This parable would not have been considered scandalous or dishonest in Jesus' day

The kingdom of heaven is like . . .

An unexpected surprise (treasure)	**An expected surprise (pearl)**
Levi the tax collector (Mark 2:14)	Simeon and Anna (Luke 2:25 – 38)
Zacchaeus (Luke 19:1–10)	John the Baptist (Matthew 3:13 –17)
Paul (Acts 9:1– 22)	

You must picture me alone in that room in Magdalen, night after night, feeling, whenever my mind lifted even for a second from my work, the steady, unrelenting approach of Him whom I so earnestly desired not to meet. That which I greatly feared had at last come upon me. In the Trinity Term of 1929 I gave in, and admitted that God was God, and knelt and prayed; perhaps, that night, the most dejected and reluctant convert in all England.

C. S. Lewis

What are you going to do when the kingdom comes?

> Unfortunately, it is all too easy to lose sight of this value and so lose the joy. This is the danger of those who grow up in fine Christian homes and good churches but who take this for granted. If a person has always known the message, he or she may not really grasp the value of the gospel.
>
> Michael Wilkins

VIDEO DISCUSSION #2

1. As a group, reflect back to when some of you first found Jesus and share whether or not it was difficult to make the decision to follow him. What kinds of changes have occurred in your lives since that day? Reflect on whether or not some of that early enthusiasm and joy of the kingdom has been lost.

2. Was your conversion to the kingdom of God more like the field hand's (an unexpected surprise) or like the pearl merchant's (an expected surprise)? Why?

CONNECTING THE BIBLE TO LIFE

The real question these parables pose is: "What are the disciples of the kingdom of heaven like?"

Video Teaching #3 Notes

These parables teach us that disciples must take action

Disciples are willing to risk

They seek first the kingdom, sacrificing all to it; but at the same time, paradoxically, they find in the kingdom all they need (Matthew 6:33).

Donald Hagner

The kingdom is far greater than any earthly treasure

Paul: But whatever was to my profit I now consider loss for the sake of Christ. What is more, I consider everything a loss compared to the surpassing greatness of knowing Christ Jesus my Lord, for whose sake I have lost all things. I consider them rubbish, that I may gain Christ and be found in him, not having a righteousness of my own that comes from the law, but that which is through faith in Christ.

Philippians 3:7–9

The kingdom of God requires a reorientation

The sacrifice of all that one has is not too much.

Leon Morris

Joy in the kingdom

We can become so familiar with the things of God that we lose sight of the incredible worth of the kingdom.

Michael Wilkins

Deepest needs met, deepest longings satisfied, deepest hurts bandaged, and a future and a hope unlike any other. It all adds up to joy.

Bruce Barton

VIDEO DISCUSSION #3

1. David Garland says that disciples must be "willing to risk everything" for the joy of the kingdom. Have you risked anything lately for the kingdom of God? What keeps us from risking more for the kingdom?

2. These parables tell us that the disciple is willing to risk everything for the kingdom because of the "joy" and surpassing "value" of the kingdom (Matthew 13:44–46). Have you found this to be true in your own life? Has the "joy of the Lord" been your strength? Would you trade what you have found in the kingdom of God for all the gold of the world? Why or why not? What have you gained in the kingdom?

3. David Garland says, "The kingdom appears in your life and it is far greater than some earthly treasure." Does this mean that we cannot have earthly treasures? Is it acceptable for the disciple of the kingdom of God to accumulate wealth (see 1 John 3:16–17)? Should the disciple be "investing" more of his/her earthly treasure in order to gain "heavenly treasure" (Matthew 6:2–4, 19–21)?

MAKING DEEPER CONNECTIONS IN YOUR OWN LIFE

Personal reflection studies to do on your own

Day One

1. Read Luke 14:25–33.

2. In the Matthew 13 parables, individuals are willing to sell *all* in order to "buy" the field or pearl (vv. 44–46). This means that the kingdom is worth more than anything that they previously owned. We often talk about sacrifice for the kingdom, but if the kingdom truly is worth more than anything else, this is not "sacrifice" but "investment." Journal briefly about the goodness of God, who showed you the worth of his kingdom and allowed you to enter into it.

3. Reflect on when you found (or were found by) God. Can you remember the emotions? Can you remember the commitments that you made in those early days? Now think about the present: are you still filled with "joy" as you walk with Jesus? Why or why not? Has something else crept in?

Day Two

1. Read Matthew 19:23–24.

2. In Dietrich Bonhoeffer's book *The Cost of Discipleship*, he talks about "cheap grace" and the tendency for people not to sacrifice for the kingdom. Is the idea of self-denying discipleship popular today (Luke 14:26–27)? Why or why not? Do you yourself struggle with this practice?

3. Reflect on the price that Jesus paid so that we can accept the free gift of salvation and enter into the kingdom. What does this tell you about the amount of love that God has for you? How valuable are you to him? How does this affect your self-image?

Day Three

1. Read Matthew 25:34.

2. While it is wonderful and helpful to consider the greatness of the kingdom of God in which we presently live, think about how much greater it will be to live in the kingdom in all its fullness — to live for an eternity in the very presence of God in heaven (1 Corinthians 2:9). How do you think it will be different from living here on earth?

3. Now that you have thought about heaven, how does the knowledge of what life will be like there affect your life here on earth? In what way does it help to change your present priorities?

Day Four

1. Read 1 John 3:16–17.

2. After reading this passage, reflect further on whether or not it is acceptable for the disciple of the kingdom of God to accumulate wealth. Is there a limit to the amount of wealth that we can have? How do we determine how we should be using our resources (Matthew 6:2–4, 19–21)?

3. What would be different in your own life and in the life of your church if you and every person in your church began to invest in heavenly things? What would this do for outreach in your community? For missions?

Day Five

1. Read Matthew 13:44–46 one more time.

2. Pray through the entire passage, allowing the deeper meaning that you have discovered to lead you as you pray. Ask the Spirit to continue to remind you of what you have learned and to help you apply these truths to your life.

3. Turn back to the discussion questions from the video teaching (Video Discussion #1, #2, #3). If there are questions that your group did not have time to discuss or questions that you might like to think more about, use this time to review and reflect further.

The Mission of the Kingdom

The Wedding Banquet (Matthew 22:1–14)

Dr. Matt Williams

"Go . . . and invite . . . anyone you find."

❧ *Matthew 22:9*

People are looking for better methods. God is looking for better people. People are God's method.

❧ *E. M. Bounds*

INTRODUCTION

Video Opener

Scripture Reading: Matthew 22:1–14, followed by a prayer that God will open your heart as you study his Word

Location of Parable: Temple courts in Jerusalem

A reconstruction of the Jerusalem temple

CONNECTING TO THE BIBLE

Royal wedding celebrations would be the event of the decade for the entire kingdom. The invited guests in this parable, however, decide not to attend. This abnormal behavior would have been very shocking to a first-century audience.

Video Teaching #1 Notes

Location of Video Teaching: Banquet hall, Temecula, California

The invitation to the banquet

In a day when people did not have watches and when banquets took a long time to prepare, they would send out a first invitation and later set the time of the banquet when everything was ready.

Leon Morris

DID YOU KNOW?

The imperfect tense of the Greek verb "refused to come" indicates that this is a repeated refusal by the invited guests.

Surprising twist: "We're not going!"

Political allegiance: king's son

The gracious king's second offer

> "Tell those who have been invited that I have prepared my dinner: My oxen and fattened cattle have been butchered, and everything is ready. Come to the wedding banquet."
>
> Matthew 22:4

Weak excuses

> "But they paid no attention and went off — one to his field, another to his business. The rest seized his servants, mistreated them and killed them."
>
> Matthew 22:5 – 6

The mistreatment of royal representatives was outright treason, constituting a declaration of revolt.

Craig Keener

Judgment

"The king was enraged. He sent his army and destroyed those murderers and burned their city."

Matthew 22:7

Go and invite the unworthy

"Then he said to his servants, 'The wedding banquet is ready, but those I invited did not deserve to come. Go to the street corners and invite to the banquet anyone you find.' So the servants went out into the streets and gathered all the people they could find, both good and bad, and the wedding hall was filled with guests."

Matthew 22:8 – 10

"Go out quickly . . . bring in the poor, the crippled, the blind and the lame."

Luke 14:21

VIDEO DISCUSSION #1

1. Looking back at the Bible passage and your video teaching notes, what did you learn that you did not know previously? Consider specifically:

   • The double invitation to banquets

   • Political allegiance

   • The grace of the king

   • "The sent one is as the sender"

   • The invitation to the unworthy

   How does this knowledge help you to understand the parable better?

2. Parables are stories told in symbolic language that sometimes refer to specific people or things. Do you think that this parable in Matthew 22 is talking about someone or something specific? Why or why not? If you think it does refer to someone specific, what do you think Jesus is trying to tell these people?

GOING DEEPER

Parables are not just stories, but stories told to make a significant point. We will not understand this point, however, if we read the parable without understanding the context of Matthew 21–22.

Video Teaching #2 Notes

The triumphal entry into Jerusalem
(Matthew 21:1–11)

> "Hosanna to the Son of David!" . . . When Jesus entered Jerusalem, the whole city was stirred.
>
> Matthew 21:9–10
>
> See, your king comes to you, righteous and having salvation, gentle and riding on a donkey.
>
> Zechariah 9:9

The cleansing of the temple (Matthew 21:12–13)

> Jesus entered the temple area and drove out all who were buying and selling there. . . . "It is written," he said to them, " 'My house will be called a house of prayer,' but you are making it a 'den of robbers.' "
>
> Matthew 21:12–13
>
> ———
>
> "Will you steal and murder, commit adultery and perjury, burn incense to Baal and follow other gods you have not known, and then come and stand before me in this house, which bears my Name, and say, 'We are safe' — safe to do all these detestable things? Has this house, which bears my Name, become a den of robbers to you? But I have been watching! declares the LORD."
>
> Jeremiah 7:9–11

The cursing of the fig tree (Matthew 21:18–22)

> When I found Israel, it was like finding grapes in the desert; when I saw your fathers, it was like seeing the early fruit on the fig tree.
>
> Hosea 9:10

Jesus has come and is ready to gather in God's people, but they are bearing no fruit at all.

Ben Witherington III

The Jewish leaders question Jesus (Matthew 21:23–27)

"By what authority are you doing these things?"

Matthew 21:23

The parable of the two sons (Matthew 21:28–32)

The parable of the tenants
(Matthew 21:33–46)

"He will bring those wretches to a wretched end," they replied, "and he will rent the vineyard to other tenants, who will give him his share of the crop at harvest time."

Matthew 21:41

"Therefore I tell you that the kingdom of God will be taken away from you and given to a people who will produce its fruit."

Matthew 21:43

Summary of Matthew 21 and Jewish messianic expectations

The parable of the wedding banquet (Matthew 22:1–14)

God is the gracious King who invites Israel to a banquet

> On this mountain the LORD Almighty will prepare a feast of rich food for all peoples, a banquet of aged wine — the best of meats and the finest of wines.
>
> Isaiah 25:6

God responds: judgment

> "The king was enraged. He sent his army and destroyed those murderers and burned their city."
>
> Matthew 22:7
>
> ———————————— ◎ ————————————
>
> "I have determined to do this city harm and not good, declares the LORD. It will be given into the hands of the king of Babylon, and he will destroy it with fire."
>
> Jeremiah 21:10

Jerusalem temple ruins

God invites the "outsiders" to respond

DID YOU KNOW?

Some think that the idea of "burning the city" found in this parable foretells what actually happens to Jerusalem, which was invaded by the Romans in AD 66 and finally destroyed with fire in AD 70.

"Go to the street corners and invite to the banquet anyone you find."

Matthew 22:9

Qumran: Everyone who is defiled in the flesh, paralyzed in his feet or hands, lame, blind, deaf, dumb . . . shall not enter to take their place among the congregation.

Rule of the Congregation 2:3 – 8

Yahweh of Hosts will make for all the peoples in this mountain a meal; and though the Gentiles suppose it is an honor, it will be a shame for them, and great plagues, plagues from which they will be unable to escape, plagues whereby they will come to their end.

Targum to Isaiah 25:6

Qumran cave IV, one of the Dead Sea Scrolls discovery sites

God is seeking a people

This is not a Jewish parable that is now Gentile; rather, it is now nonethnic. The church includes both Jew and Gentile.

W. D. Davies and Dale C. Allison

VIDEO DISCUSSION #2

1. How has understanding the contents of Matthew 21 helped you to better understand the parable of the wedding banquet in Matthew 22?

2. From this passage, do you think that God is gracious or a tyrant? Cite specific verses from Matthew 21–22 as evidence for your answer.

3. Imagine that you are in Jesus' audience as he tells these parables. What would your reaction be if you were a Pharisee? If you were a common person? Why do you think you would react that way?

CONNECTING THE BIBLE TO LIFE

God invited the Jewish people to the banquet of his Son, Jesus the Messiah. Some rejected the offer, so God extends the kingdom to all people who respond with fruit.

Video Teaching #3 Notes

The kind of people God seeks

First fruit: "dressed" properly

Those who respond to the King must change their lives

DID YOU KNOW?

The term "friend" in verse 12 is not friendly, but a term used in Matthew for false disciples (20:13; 26:50).

"But when the king came in to see the guests, he noticed a man there who was not wearing wedding clothes. 'Friend,' he asked, 'how did you get in here without wedding clothes?' The man was speechless. Then the king told the attendants, 'Tie him hand and foot, and throw him outside, into the darkness, where there will be weeping and gnashing of teeth.'"

Matthew 22:11–13

Clothes were available for the banquet

"Clothes" are available to us today

> "As a prisoner for the Lord, then, I urge you to live a life worthy of the calling you have received."
>
> Ephesians 4:1

Wedding garments are often equated with [doing] good works . . . of righteousness, as we see in Revelation 19:7–8: "Let us rejoice and be glad and give him glory! For the wedding of the Lamb has come, and his bride has made herself ready. Fine linen, bright and clean, was given her to wear."

W. D. Davies and Dale C. Allison

God is a gracious God who invites those who are not worthy into his banquet to feast with him. He does not, though, accept our sinful lifestyle but calls us to repentance and transformation.

Matt Williams

Second fruit: "Go to the street corners and invite to the banquet anyone you find" (Matthew 22:9)

Old Testament evangelism/missions

"The LORD rises upon you and his glory appears over you. Nations will come to your light."

Isaiah 60:2–3

Jesus' emphasis on evangelism/missions (Matthew 28:18–20)

The mission now becomes centrifugal instead of centripetal. This means that instead of the Gentiles coming to Israel to hear God's message, Jesus' disciples are to go to all the nations with the gospel.

Michael Wilkins

VIDEO DISCUSSION #3

1. Matt Williams said, "Those who respond to the King must change their lives." Read 2 Peter 1:10. There are some in today's church who think that simply by attending church services, they have responded adequately to the King's invitation. How would you respond to these people based on Matthew 22?

2. Do you think that the churches in your community are more "centrifugal" (going out to seek the lost) or "centripetal" (letting the lost come to them)? Give an example or two, then draw on your Bible knowledge to note specific verses in the New Testament that teach both methods.

3. This parable tells us to "Go . . . and invite . . . anyone you find" (Matthew 22:9). In the first century they would have found and invited Jews, Romans, Canaanites, the lame, the poor, the rich — the same type of diversity that we see in the early church. What about us today? Do we focus our ministries on just one segment of the population — just one race, just the rich, just the poor, and so on — or do we go and invite ALL to God's table?

MAKING DEEPER CONNECTIONS IN YOUR OWN LIFE

Personal reflection studies to do on your own

Day One

1. Read Luke 14:15–24, noting the similarities to and differences from Matthew 22:1–14.

2. If you were living in the first century, do you think that you would have responded to this invitation to the wedding banquet of the King's Son, Jesus the Messiah? Why or why not?

3. Just as the invited guests in this parable said no to the king because they were too busy (Matthew 22:5), we do the same today. We are too busy to pray, to "go and invite," to show hospitality, to help the needy. Sometimes we need to learn to say no to good things so that we can say yes to better things. Is your life too busy? What might you be missing out on because of your busyness?

4. The video teaching in this study spoke at length about the context of Matthew 21 in order to correctly understand this parable in Matthew 22. Do you think that the church today reads biblical accounts within their context, or do we just read individual passages with little regard to the context? What happens when we interpret the Bible in this way?

Day Two

1. Read Ezekiel 36:25–27 and Romans 8:1–11.

2. As the Matthew parable shows, those who respond to the King must wear the proper "clothes." Thankfully, unlike those who responded to God in the Old Testament, we now have the "promised Holy Spirit" (Ephesians 1:13) to empower us to change. Using the texts of Ezekiel 36:25–27 and Romans 8:1–11, ask the Spirit to empower you to overcome those areas of difficulty in your life (write them down here) so that you can say yes to God's invitation.

3. Read 1 Peter 4:16–19 and 2 Peter 1:10. Journal briefly about the attitude of spiritual smugness sometimes found in the church or in your own life. These passages in Peter, along with our parable, remind us of the need to make sure that we are responding properly to the King as we walk through this life. It is not just a one-time decision in the past, but a lifetime of saying yes to the King's invitation to follow him.

Day Three

1. Read Luke 14:25–33.

2. Sometimes the invitation to the wedding banquet of Jesus is presented in a very simple fashion, sometimes as an intellectual decision that one needs to make. Jesus, on the other hand, taught that one should consider the cost of commitment very carefully. From your reading of Luke 14:25–33, think about how you invite others to the banquet of Jesus. Do you need to change anything in your approach?

3. This parable in Matthew 22 also teaches us that Jesus' harshest criticism and judgment were for the "insiders," those he initially invited. This should cause us to stop and reflect on our own lives. Have we in the church become calloused to God's invitation and the response that it requires?

Day Four

1. Read Matthew 23.

2. Though we seldom talk about it in our politically correct world, the Matthew 22 parable teaches about the reality of judgment for those who do not respond properly (v. 13). Read what Jesus says to the Pharisees and teachers of the law in Matthew 23. Do you think that this kind of teaching should be part of our ministry today? Why or why not? If not, how can we talk about the reality of judgment in a world that does not believe in such a thing?

3. Jesus the Jewish Messiah announces judgment first on those within Israel who do not produce the proper fruit (Matthew 21:43), and then on "anyone" (Jew or Gentile) who seems to respond to his invitation, but does not wear the proper "clothes." This is not a parable that is anti-Judaism, but rather anti-hypocrisy. If God were examining your life today, would he be able to find any hypocrisy? If so, in what area? How might you counteract it?

Day Five

1. Read Matthew 22:1–14 one more time.

2. Pray through the entire passage verse by verse, allowing the deeper meaning that you have discovered to lead you as you pray. Ask the Spirit to continue to remind you of what you have learned and to help you apply these truths to your life.

3. Turn back to the discussion questions from the video teaching (Video Discussion #1, #2, #3). If there are questions that your group did not have time to discuss or questions that you might like to think more about, use this time to review and reflect further.

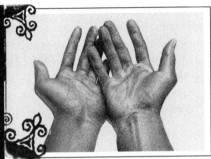

The Fulfillment of the Kingdom

Sheep and Goats (Matthew 25:31–46)

Dr. Mark Strauss

"All the nations will be gathered before him, and he will separate the people one from another as a shepherd separates the sheep from the goats."

Matthew 25:32

God is calling us to let go of our resources and to turn them over for his service.

Mark Strauss

INTRODUCTION

Video Opener

Scripture Reading: Matthew 25:31–46, followed by a prayer that God will open your heart as you study his Word

Location of Parable: Mount of Olives, Jerusalem

Mount of Olives

CONNECTING TO THE BIBLE

If God is good and all-powerful, why does he allow bad things to happen? Theologians and philosophers call this "the problem of evil."

Video Teaching #1 Notes

Location of Video Teaching: A park near San Diego, California

Disasters: the problem of evil

Hurricane Katrina damage

Why doesn't God fix it now?

The Olivet Discourse, Matthew 24–25

The Son of Man will judge

"In my vision at night I looked, and there before me was one like a son of man, coming with the clouds of heaven. He approached the Ancient of Days and was led into his presence. He was given authority, glory and sovereign power."

Daniel 7:13–14

Jesus functions as the judge — a role restricted to God in the Old Testament.

Donald Hagner

Sheep on the right and goats on the left

DID YOU KNOW?

The goats in Palestinian flocks are hard to distinguish from the sheep, which are not like the white varieties of Europe.

R. T. France

The Lord is my shepherd.   Psalm 23:1

———————————————— ☙ ————————————————

"I am the good shepherd; I know my sheep and my sheep know me."

John 10:14

Flock of sheep in Israel

Goat in that same flock

The sheep inherit the kingdom

"The King will reply, 'I tell you the truth, whatever you did for one of the least of these brothers of mine, you did for me.'"

Matthew 25:40

- You gave me something to eat when I was hungry. (v. 35)
- You gave me something to drink when I was thirsty. (v. 35)
- You invited me in when I was a stranger. (v. 35)
- You clothed me when I was naked. (v. 36)
- You looked after me when I was sick. (v. 36)
- You came to visit me when I was in prison. (v. 36)

The goats are sent into the eternal fire

"Whatever you did not do for one of the least of these, you did not do for me."

Matthew 25:45

I did not prepare the fire for you but for the devil and his angels. But you have cast yourselves in it. Even when you see a dog hungry, you feel sympathy. But when you see the Lord hungry, you ignore it. You are left without excuse.

Chrysostom, an early church father

Our eternal destiny is connected to how we treat others

Now is the time to "seek the Lord while he may be found," for the God of grace will judge the world.

Robert Stein

VIDEO DISCUSSION #1

1. Looking back at the Bible passage and your video teaching notes, what did you learn that you did not know previously? Consider specifically:

   • The problem of evil

   • The "high Christology," with Jesus as the Judge

   • The "right" versus the "left"

   • The reason for the reward or judgment

   How does this knowledge help you to understand the parable better?

2. The "problem of evil" is the biggest stumbling block that non-Christians have with Christianity's claim that God is good. Have you had any such conversations with non-Christians? What did you say to them? Have you yourself ever struggled with this problem? If so, what did you do? How can we as Christians better respond to these questions?

3. Does it surprise you that this parable tells us that the sheep and the goats will be divided based upon what they "did" or "did not do" (Matthew 25:40, 45)? Why or why not?

GOING DEEPER

How we act toward other members of the body of Christ reflects our attitude toward Jesus himself. As Matthew 25 reminds us, "Whatever you did for one of the least of these brothers of mine, you did for me."

Video Teaching #2 Notes

Who are the "least of these"?

Neighbors: As we have opportunity, let us do good to all people.

Galatians 6:10

Christian Believers: "For whoever does the will of my Father in heaven is my brother and sister and mother."

Matthew 12:50

Evangelists/Missionaries: "If anyone gives even a cup of cold water to one of these little ones because he is my disciple, I tell you the truth, he will certainly not lose his reward."

Matthew 10:42

One's fate will be determined by how one responds to Jesus' followers who are charged with spreading the gospel and do so in the face of hunger, thirst, illness and imprisonment.

D. A. Carson

Do we earn salvation by *doing* good deeds?

Paul: For it is by grace you have been saved, through faith — and this not from yourselves, it is the gift of God — not by works.

Ephesians 2:8–9

James: You see that a person is justified by what he does and not by faith alone.

James 2:24

Resolving the tension between faith and works

We are saved by faith alone, but the kind of faith that saves is never alone.

Robert Stein

Transformation

Therefore, if anyone is in Christ, he is a new creation; the old has gone, the new has come!

2 Corinthians 5:17

We are not saved because we do works; rather we do works because we've been saved by and transformed through Christ.

Mark Strauss

The nature of the judgment

Eternal life

Eternal punishment: hell

O sinner! Consider the fearful danger you are in: it is a great furnace of wrath, a wide and bottomless pit, full of the fire of wrath, that you are held over in the hand of that God. . . . You hang by a slender thread, with the flames of divine wrath flashing about it, and ready every moment to singe it, and burn it asunder.

Jonathan Edwards, colonial American preacher

Fire: real or metaphorical

Could it be that the fire Jesus talked about is an eternal search for God that is never quenched? That, indeed, would be hell. To be away from God forever, separated from his presence.

Billy Graham

The key purpose of this passage

VIDEO DISCUSSION #2

1. Mark Strauss has argued that the "least of these" refers to Christians, and probably to evangelists and missionaries who spread the Christian message. Read Matthew 10:5–7, 40–42. Do you think that this passage helps us to understand who the "least of these" are in Matthew 25? Why or why not?

2. Why do you think many churchgoers do not have good works to pair with their "faith"? What helps you to understand the relationship between faith and works?

3. Why do you think that people today do not discuss God's judgment or hell very much (Matthew 25:41, 46)? Though judgment and hell are controversial topics, how can they be used positively to advance the gospel?

CONNECTING THE BIBLE TO LIFE

Jesus' teaching reminds us that there are eternal consequences for our actions.

Video Teaching #3 Notes

Be consistent

> The presence of kingdom life will always produce evidence in the transformed speech, thought, actions, and character of Jesus' followers.
>
> Michael Wilkins

Be ready

> "Do not store up for yourselves treasures on earth, where moth and rust destroy, and where thieves break in and steal. But store up for yourselves treasures in heaven."
>
> Matthew 6:19–20

Live in the present with one eye toward the future.

Be responsible

Be compassionate

Needy disciples are often the ones who are excluded from care — attention is often wrongfully diverted to prominent members of the discipleship community.

Michael Wilkins

Knowing that our time on earth is just a moment, knowing that judgment is coming should change the way we live, should change the way we use the resources God has given us.

Mark Strauss

VIDEO DISCUSSION #3

1. Mark Strauss talked about the transformation of a caterpillar to a butterfly to illustrate how the Christian has also been transformed (2 Corinthians 5:17). The Christian, by nature, should show evidence of the types of good works listed in the Matthew 25 passage. What would you say about the "Christian" who does not evidence the character traits that Mark Strauss outlined in the video: consistency, readiness, responsibility, and compassion? Is it normal to be lacking in these areas?

2. Which of the four character traits that Mark Strauss mentioned does today's church most struggle with?

3. Just as it would be unthinkable for someone to play with the fire engine that came to put out the fire in their burning house, Mark Strauss said that it is inconsistent when Chris- tians blessed with many resources do not help others. Read Matthew 6:19–20. Do you think that Christians today are "playing" with their resources, or are they investing them in "eternal" things?

MAKING DEEPER CONNECTIONS IN YOUR OWN LIFE

Personal reflection studies to do on your own

Day One

1. Read Colossians 3:1–17.

2. Mark Strauss said, "Knowing that our time on earth is just a moment and that judgment is coming should change the way we live and change the way we use the resources God has given us." Reflect on whether or not *you* are using your resources the way that God would want you to use them. Ask him to show you areas where you might be accumulating instead of investing in eternal things.

3. If it is true that the Matthew 25 parable teaches us that at the final judgment God will look at the good deeds that we Christians have *done* for other Christians, especially evangelists and missionaries, why do you think that the church today is not showing more interest in the ministries of evangelism and missions? (For example, it often takes more than two years for missionaries to raise the support that they need to go to the mission field.)

4. Journal briefly about the specifics of what it means in our daily life to set our hearts and minds "on things above" (Colossians 3:2). Compare this passage in Colossians to the parable in Matthew 25:31–46.

Day Two

1. Read 2 Corinthians 5:9–11.

2. The Matthew 25 parable reminds us that there are only two kinds of people: the blessed and the cursed (vv. 31–33). Sometimes we Christians forget that the future of our neighbors might be eternal punishment. Jesus speaks often about the love of God, but he also teaches about the holiness of God. Reflect on these two natures of God and what that means for those people in your life who still do not know Jesus as their Messiah.

3. A former neighbor of mine used to say that he would repent when he was older. A former boss used to tell me that he would follow God later, he just wasn't ready yet. Matthew 25:31 reminds us of the suddenness of the return of the Son of Man. Remember the apostle Paul's words in 2 Corinthians 6:2: "Now is the day of salvation." Reflect on your life and whether or not you are doing all you can to show others — through your actions and through your words — that the King will return suddenly in judgment to reward and to punish.

Day Three

1. Read 1 Corinthians 4:1–5.

2. We often think that it is the rich who really can affect the ministry of God in the world with their large and influential gifts. The Matthew 25 parable reminds us that it is the smallest and simplest acts that make a difference in our world. Not only are we helping those with whom we share our resources (time, talents, treasures), but we are also witnessing to those around us that God has been good to us and has transformed our naturally selfish nature (Matthew 5:16). Write down some of the "little things" you could do today that might make a huge difference in your world.

3. Jesus tells the sheep, "Take your inheritance, the kingdom prepared for you since the creation of the world" (Matthew 25:34). Revelation 21:7 says, "He who overcomes will inherit all this," which refers to the beautiful city of New Jerusalem. The idea of inheriting the riches of God and reigning with him has been God's plan from the beginning (Genesis 1:26: "let them rule over"). It is also clear from Scripture that God will only give us more resources if we show that we are responsible with those that we already have (Matthew 25:21). If God were to judge your life today, do you think he would conclude that you are using your resources well or that you could use them more efficiently? Explain.

Day Four

1. Read 2 Peter 3:1–14.

2. The Matthew 25 parable does not *answer* the "problem of evil," but it shows that Jesus was fully aware of the problem and would address it at the end of the age. In the meantime, we can rest assured that God is gracious in the delay of the second coming. Reread 2 Peter 3:9 and journal briefly about what God might be doing in the world today as we await the end.

3. The Matthew 25 parable also reminds us that we must share the gospel with urgency, boldness, and clarity, along with humility, gentleness, and love. We should hide neither heaven nor hell as we tell others about God. Reflect on how you share the portion of the gospel message that deals with our eternal destiny. Does this parable help you to formulate your view better? Why or why not?

Day Five

1. Read Matthew 25:31–46 one more time.

2. Pray through the entire passage verse by verse, allowing the deeper meaning that you have discovered to lead you as you pray. Ask the Spirit to continue to remind you of what you have learned and to help you apply these truths to your life.

3. Turn back to the discussion questions from the video teaching (Video Discussion #1, #2, #3). If there are questions that your group did not have time to discuss or questions that you might like to think more about, use this time to review and reflect further.

Source Acknowledgments

(These are noted in order of appearance for each session. When quoted from a commentary, full source information can be found in "Books for Further Reading" beginning on page 133.)

Session One

Page 11: Blomberg, *Matthew*, 221.
Page 15: France, *Matthew*, 225.
Page 15: Davies and Allison, *Matthew*, 408.
Page 16: Mounce, *Matthew*, 132.
Page 21: Morris, *Matthew*, 351.
Page 23: Wilkins, *Matthew*, 503.
Page 24: Ibid., 504.
Page 24: Hagner (in Longenecker), *Challenge of Jesus' Parables*, 112.

Session Two

Page 31: Morris, *Luke*, 163.
Page 34: Strauss, *Bible Backgrounds Commentary*, 388.
Page 35: Green, *Luke*, 313.
Page 36: Morris, *Luke*, 162.
Page 38: Bock, *Luke*, 694.
Page 39: Morris, *Luke*, 161.
Page 39: Keener, *Bible Background Commentary*, 209.
Page 40: Green, *Luke*, 314.
Page 40: Strauss, *Bible Backgrounds Commentary*, 389.
Page 41: Morris, *Luke*, 163.

Session Three

Page 49: Bailey, *Poet and Peasant*, 205.
Page 51: Strauss, *Bible Backgrounds Commentary*, 447.
Page 51: Evans, *Luke*, 411.
Page 52: Liefeld, *Luke*, 984.
Page 53: Nolland, *Luke*, 786.

Page 53: Strauss, *Bible Backgrounds Commentary*, 448.
Page 56: Bailey, *Poet and Peasant*, 161–62.
Page 56: Strauss, *Bible Backgrounds Commentary*, 447.
Page 56: Bailey, *Poet and Peasant*, 168.
Page 57: Nolland, *Luke*, 780.
Page 58: Strauss, *Bible Backgrounds Commentary*, 448.
Page 58: Keener, *Bible Background Commentary*, 233.
Page 59: Bailey, *Poet and Peasant*, 182.
Page 61: Ibid., 187.
Page 64: Tomlin, "Come Home Running," © 2002 sixsteprecords.

Session Four

Page 69: Hagner, *Matthew*, 397.
Page 72: Wilkins, *Matthew*, 488.
Page 75: C. S. Lewis, *Surprised by Joy: The Shape of My Early Life*, New York: Harcourt, Brace and World, 1955, 228.
Page 76: Wilkins, *Matthew*, 505.
Page 77: Hagner, *Matthew*, 397.
Page 78: Morris, *Matthew*, 360.
Page 79: Wilkins, *Matthew*, 505.
Page 79: Barton, *Matthew*, 274.

Session Five

Page 85: Bounds, *The Complete Works of E. M. Bounds on Prayer*.
Page 87: Morris, *Matthew*, 548.
Page 88: Keener, *Bible Background Commentary*, 104.
Page 92: Witherington III, *Mark*, 313.
Page 96: Davies and Allison, *Matthew*, 204.
Page 99: Ibid.
Page 100: Wilkins, *Matthew*, 706.

Session Six

Page 110: Hagner, *Matthew*, 742.
Page 110: France, *Matthew*, 356.
Page 112: Chrysostom, *Matthew*, Homily, 79.2.
Page 112: Stein, *Parables of Jesus*, 130.
Page 115: Carson, *Matthew, Mark, Luke*, 520.
Page 116: Stein, *Parables of Jesus*, 136.
Page 117: Jonathan Edwards, "Sinners in the Hands of an Angry God."
Page 118: Billy Graham, *The Challenge*, Garden City, N.Y.: Doubleday, 1969, 75.
Page 120: Wilkins, *Matthew*, 813.
Page 121: Ibid., 811.

Map and Photo Credits

Maps: © Michael Schmeling www.aridocean.com

Franz Rigsby Dunn: page 16

McRay Ritmyer Konstas: page 20

T. J. Rathbun: pages 61, 62, 86, 96 (top), 108, 111

Zondervan Image Archives (Neal Bierling): pages 12, 35, 70, 95

iStockphoto.com: pages 11, 14, 23, 24, 31, 33, 34, 38, 39 (bottom), 42, 58, 60, 69, 71, 72, 75, 77, 85, 89, 93, 96 (bottom), 100, 107, 109, 110, 116, 118

shutterstock.com: pages 19, 39 (top), 49, 52, 91, 98, 121

Books for Further Reading

Four Gospels

Evans, Craig A., gen. ed. *The Bible Knowledge Background Commentary: Matthew – Luke.* Colorado Springs: Victor Books, 2003.

Keener, Craig S. *The IVP Bible Background Commentary: New Testament.* Downers Grove, Ill.: InterVarsity Press, 1993.

Matthew

Barton, Bruce B. *Matthew.* Life Application Bible Commentary. Wheaton, Ill.: Tyndale, 1996.

Blomberg, Craig L. *Matthew.* New American Commentary, vol. 22. Nashville: Broadman, 1992.

Carson, D. A. *Matthew, Mark, Luke.* The Expositor's Bible Commentary, vol. 8. Grand Rapids, Mich.: Zondervan, 1984.

_____. *When Jesus Confronts the World: An Exposition of Matthew 8 – 10.* Grand Rapids, Mich.: Baker, 1987.

Davies, W. D. and Dale C. Allison, Jr. *A Critical and Exegetical Commentary on the Gospel According to Saint Matthew.* The International Critical Commentary. 3 vols. Edinburgh: T. & T. Clark, 1988, 1991, 1997.

France, R. T. *The Gospel According to Matthew: An Introduction and Commentary.* Tyndale New Testament Commentaries, vol. 1. Grand Rapids, Mich.: Eerdmans, 1985.

Green, Michael. *The Message of Matthew: The Kingdom of Heaven.* The Bible Speaks Today Series. Downers Grove, Ill.: InterVarsity Press, 2000.

Guelich, Robert A. *Sermon on the Mount: A Foundation for Understanding.* Waco, Tex.: Word, 1982.

Gundry, Robert. *Matthew: A Commentary on His Handbook for a Mixed Church Under Persecution.* Grand Rapids, Mich.: Eerdmans, 2nd ed. 1994.

Hagner, Donald. *Matthew.* Word Biblical Commentary, vol. 33a – b. Waco, Tex.: Word, 1993, 1995.

Keener, Craig S. *A Commentary on the Gospel of Matthew*. Grand Rapids, Mich.: Eerdmans, 1999.

Morris, Leon. *The Gospel According to Matthew. The Pillar New Testament Commentary*. Grand Rapids, Mich.: Eerdmans, 1992.

Mounce, Robert H. *Matthew*. New International Biblical Commentary, vol. 1. Peabody, Mass.: Hendrickson, 1991.

Nolland, John. *The Gospel of Matthew: A Commentary on the Greek Text*. The New International Greek Testament Commentary. Grand Rapids, Mich.: Eerdmans, 2005.

Simonetti, Manlio, ed. *Matthew*. Ancient Christian Commentary on Scripture. 2 vols. Downers Grove, Ill.: InterVarsity Press, 2002.

Turner, David and Darrell L. Bock. *Matthew, Mark*. Cornerstone Biblical Commentary. Wheaton, Ill.: Tyndale, 2006.

Wilkins, Michael J. *Matthew*. The NIV Application Commentary. Grand Rapids, Mich.: Zondervan, 2004.

_____. *Zondervan Illustrated Bible Backgrounds Commentary*, vol. 1. Grand Rapids, Mich.: Zondervan, 2002.

Mark

Cole, R. Alan. *The Gospel According to Mark*. Tyndale New Testament Commentaries, vol. 2. Grand Rapids, Mich.: Eerdmans, 2002.

Cranfield, C. E. B. *The Gospel According to Saint Mark: An Introduction and Commentary*. Cambridge Greek Testament Commentary. Cambridge, England: Cambridge University Press, 1972.

Edwards, James R. *The Gospel According to Mark*. The Pillar New Testament Commentary. Grand Rapids, Mich.: Eerdmans, 2002.

Evans, Craig. *Mark*. Word Biblical Commentary, vol. 34b. Nashville: Thomas Nelson, 2001.

Fackler, Mark. *Mark*. Life Application Bible Commentary. Wheaton, Ill.: Tyndale, 1994.

France, R. T. *The Gospel of Mark: A Commentary on the Greek Text*. The New International Greek New Testament Commentary. Grand Rapids, Mich.: Eerdmans, 2002.

Garland, David E. *Mark*. The NIV Application Commentary. Grand Rapids, Mich.: Zondervan, 1996.

_____. *Zondervan Illustrated Bible Backgrounds Commentary*, vol. 1. Grand Rapids, Mich.: Zondervan, 2002.

Guelich, Robert A. *Mark*. Word Biblical Commentary, vol. 34a. Dallas: Word, 1989.

Gundry, Robert H. *Mark: A Commentary on His Apology for the Cross*. Grand Rapids, Mich.: Eerdmans, 1993.

Lane, William L. *The Gospel According to Mark: The English Text with Introduction, Exposition, and Notes.* The New International Commentary on the New Testament. Grand Rapids, Mich.: Eerdmans, 1974.

Mann, C. S. *Mark: A New Translation with Introduction and Commentary.* Garden City, N.Y.: Doubleday, 1986.

Oden, Thomas C. and Christopher A. Hall, eds. *Mark.* Ancient Christian Commentary on Scripture, vol. 2. Downers Grove, Ill.: InterVarsity Press, 1998.

Taylor, Vincent. *The Gospel According to St. Mark: The Greek Text with Introduction, Notes, and Indexes.* Thornapple Commentaries. Grand Rapids, Mich.: Baker, 2nd ed. 1981.

Wessel, Walter W. *Matthew, Mark, Luke.* The Expositor's Bible Commentary, vol. 8. Grand Rapids, Mich.: Zondervan, 1984.

Witherington, Ben III. *The Gospel of Mark: A Socio-Rhetorical Commentary.* Grand Rapids, Mich.: Eerdmans, 2001.

Luke

Barton, Bruce B., Dave Veerman, and Linda K. Taylor. *Luke.* Life Application Bible Commentary. Wheaton, Ill.: Tyndale, 1997.

Bock, Darrell L. *Luke.* The NIV Application Commentary. Grand Rapids, Mich.: Zondervan, 1996.

Evans, Craig A. *Luke.* New International Biblical Commentary, vol. 3. Peabody, Mass.: Hendrickson, 1990.

Fitzmyer, J. A. *The Gospel According to Luke: Introduction, Translation, and Notes.* Anchor Bible, vol. 28 – 28a. Garden City, N.Y.: Doubleday, 1981 – 1985.

Green, Joel B. *The Gospel of Luke.* New International Commentary on the New Testament. Grand Rapids, Mich.: Eerdmans, 1997.

Just, Arther A. Jr., ed. *Luke.* Ancient Christian Commentary on Scripture, vol. 3. Downers Grove, Ill.: InterVarsity Press, 2003.

Liefeld, Walter L. *Matthew, Mark, Luke.* The Expositor's Bible Commentary, vol. 8. Grand Rapids, Mich.: Zondervan, 1984.

Marshall, I. Howard. *Luke: Historian and Theologian.* Grand Rapids, Mich.: Zondervan, 1980.

Morris, Leon. *Luke: An Introduction and Commentary.* Tyndale New Testament Commentaries, vol. 3. Grand Rapids, Mich.: Eerdmans, 1988.

Nolland, John. *Luke.* Word Biblical Commentary, vol. 35a – c. Dallas: Word, 1989 – 1993.

Stein, Robert H. *Luke.* The New American Commentary, vol. 24. Nashville: Broadman, 1992.

Strauss, Mark L. *Zondervan Illustrated Bible Backgrounds Commentary*, vol. 1. Grand Rapids, Mich.: Zondervan, 2002.

John

Barrett, C. K. *The Gospel According to St. John: An Introduction with Commentary and Notes on the Greek Text*. Philadelphia: Westminster Press, 1978.

Barton, Bruce B. *John*. Life Application Bible Commentary. Wheaton, Ill.: Tyndale, 1993.

Beasley-Murray, George R. *John*. Word Biblical Commentaries, vol. 36. Nashville: Thomas Nelson, 1999.

Brown, Raymond Edward. *The Gospel According to John*. Anchor Bible, vol. 29–29a. Garden City, N.Y.: Doubleday, 1966–1970.

Burge, Gary M. *John*. The NIV Application Commentary. Grand Rapids, Mich.: Zondervan, 2000.

Card, Michael. *The Parable of Joy: Reflections on the Wisdom of the Book of John*. Nashville: Thomas Nelson, 1995.

Carson, D. A. *The Gospel According to John*. The Pillar New Testament Commentary. Grand Rapids, Mich.: Eerdmans, 1991.

Keener, Craig S. *The Gospel of John: A Commentary*. 2 vols. Peabody, Mass.: Hendrickson, 2003.

Köstenberger, Andreas J. John. Baker Exegetical Commentary on the New Testament. Grand Rapids, Mich.: Baker, 2004.

_____. *Zondervan Illustrated Bible Backgrounds Commentary*, vol. 2. Grand Rapids, Mich.: Zondervan, 2002.

Morris, Leon. *The Gospel According to John*. New International Commentary on the New Testament. Grand Rapids, Mich.: Eerdmans, 1995.

Tasker, R. V. G. *The Gospel According to St. John: An Introduction and Commentary*. Tyndale New Testament Commentaries. Grand Rapids, Mich.: Eerdmans, 1960.

Tenney, Merrill C. *John, Acts*. The Expositor's Bible Commentary, vol. 9. Grand Rapids, Mich.: Zondervan, 1984.

Whitacre, Rodney A. *John*. The IVP New Testament Commentary Series, vol. 4. Downers Grove, Ill.: InterVarsity Press, 1999.

Parables

Bailey, Kenneth E. *Poet and Peasant* and *Through Peasant Eyes: A Literary-Cultural Approach to the Parables in Luke*. Grand Rapids, Mich.: Eerdmans, 1983.

Blomberg, Craig L. *Interpreting the Parables*. Downers Grove, Ill.: InterVarsity Press, 1990.

Jeremias, Joachim. *The Parables of Jesus*, rev. ed. New York: Scribner, 1963.

Longenecker, Richard N., ed. The Challenge of Jesus' Parables. Grand Rapids, Mich.: Eerdmans, 2000.

Stein, Robert H. *An Introduction to the Parables of Jesus*. Philadelphia: Westminster Press, 1981.

Wenham, David. *The Parables of Jesus*. Downers Grove, Ill.: InterVarsity Press 1989.